Trading Gold

Madelyn Price

Madelyn Price

Copyright Page

Index

Introduction to the Gold Market — 7

The Dynamics of Gold Price — 13

How to Invest in Physical Gold — 20

Trading Gold in the Futures Market — 27

Trading Gold Through ETFs and Funds — 34

Gold Trading in the Forex Market — 42

The Role of Gold in a Diversified Portfolio — 50

Technical Analysis for Gold Trading — 58

Fundamental Analysis of the Gold Market — 67

The Impact of Central Banks on the Price of Gold — 75

Gold Trading During Economic Crises — 83

The Effect of Geopolitics on the Gold Market — 91

Gold Trading Secrets for Success — 99

How to Get Rich Trading Gold — 107

Introduction to the Gold Market

Gold has been considered one of the most valuable and trusted assets throughout history. From ancient civilizations to the modern world, this precious metal has captured the imagination of mankind, not only for its beauty, but also for its ability to retain value. Throughout the centuries, gold has played a pivotal role in the global economy. For centuries, it was used as a currency of exchange and today it remains a safe haven for investors in times of economic uncertainty.

The main reason why gold is so important is due to its stability. Unlike other forms of investment, such as stocks or real estate, gold is not dependent on the performance of a company or the economy of a particular country. Gold has an intrinsic value that has proven to be resilient in the face of economic fluctuations. This means that when financial markets fall or economies face difficulties, many people turn to gold to protect their money. It is common to hear that when there is a crisis, investors "run to gold," and it is precisely for this reason: it is an asset that, over time, has maintained its value even in the worst of times.

One of the most interesting aspects of the gold market is how its price fluctuates. Although at first glance it may seem that gold always has the same value, the reality is that its price changes daily, influenced by multiple factors. Inflation, for example, is one of the main reasons why gold can increase in price. When money loses value due to inflation, gold tends to appreciate, as people perceive it as a safer way to store wealth. In addition, decisions by governments and central banks also have a major impact. If central banks decide to buy more gold for their reserves, this can cause the price to rise due to increased demand.

Another key aspect of gold is its ability to resist depreciation. Unlike cash or coins, which can quickly lose value due to inflation or economic policies, gold has maintained its value over the centuries. Even in times of hyperinflation or currency crises, gold remains a reliable source of wealth. This makes it an attractive option not only for large investors, but also for ordinary people looking to protect their wealth.

Throughout history, gold has been a symbol of power and wealth. Ancient civilizations such as the Egyptians, Greeks, and Romans used gold in their coins and jewelry, recognizing its durability and rarity. In more recent times, during the 19th and 20th centuries, gold was the basis of the monetary system known as the gold standard, where the value of money was directly backed by gold reserves. Although this system is no longer used today, gold remains a key element in global finance.

Today, the gold market is global and encompasses many forms of investment. Not only is it possible to buy physical gold, such as bullion or coins, but one can also invest in gold through financial markets, such as futures or exchange-traded funds (ETFs). This has made it easier for more people to access the gold market without needing to own the physical metal. However, even with these developments, gold is still seen by many as the safest option in times of economic instability.

One of the reasons gold is so important in the modern world is its safe haven status. When stock markets fall or economies face turmoil, investors tend to sell their stocks and buy gold. This phenomenon has been evident in several recent economic crises, such as the 2008 financial crisis or the uncertainty generated by the pandemic in 2020. In both cases, the price of gold rose significantly as investors sought to protect their money against the volatility of other assets.

Gold also has a unique relationship with currencies and interest rates. Generally, when interest rates are low, the price of gold tends to rise. This is because investors find it less attractive to keep their money in deposits or bonds that offer low returns, so they prefer to invest in gold. At the same time, when a currency is devalued, as has happened in some developing countries, gold becomes more valuable in terms of that currency.

In short, the gold market is fascinating and complex. Although it appears to be a simple metal, its implications for the global economy and finance are enormous. Not only has gold been a symbol of wealth for thousands of years, but it also continues to be a vital tool for investors seeking stability and protection from the ups and downs of the financial world. Understanding how this market works and why gold is so valuable is the first step to becoming a successful trader in this exciting world.

The Dynamics of Gold Price

The price of gold is like a mirror that reflects what is happening in the world. Although it often seems that gold always has the same value, the reality is that its price is constantly changing. These price changes are influenced by a variety of factors, some more predictable than others, and understanding these dynamics is key for anyone who wants to trade in the gold market. Throughout this chapter, we will explore how and why the price of gold rises or falls, and how traders can take advantage of these movements to their advantage.

One of the main factors that affects the price of gold is inflation. Inflation is basically when the cost of things goes up and money loses purchasing power. During times when inflation is high, gold tends to go up in price. This happens because people are looking for a way to protect their money, since what they could buy with a bill a year ago now costs more, but the value of gold remains strong. During such times, many investors see gold as a way to store wealth without it losing value. For example, if you have a gold bar, no matter how high inflation is, that gold will retain its value and will probably even appreciate over time.

Another factor that has a major impact on the price of gold is supply and demand. Like any other commodity, when there is more demand than supply, the price rises. This can happen, for example, when central banks decide to buy large amounts of gold for their reserves. These moves often cause the price of gold to rise, because with less gold available on the market, the remaining gold becomes more valuable. It can also happen that gold production at mines is affected by problems such as strikes or natural disasters. If suddenly less gold is produced, the supply decreases and prices rise.

Geopolitics also plays a major role in the dynamics of the gold price. In times of political tension, such as wars or conflicts between countries, gold tends to rise. This is because gold is seen as a safe haven in times of uncertainty. When the future seems uncertain, many investors prefer to have their money in something as solid and durable as gold rather than risk it in stocks or currencies that could lose value due to political instability. A clear example of this was during the global financial crisis of 2008, when the price of gold reached historic levels as people sought to protect their money amid economic chaos.

Interest rates also have a very interesting relationship with the price of gold. Generally, when interest rates are low, the price of gold tends to rise. This happens because investors do not find it attractive to leave their money in savings accounts or bonds that offer low returns. Instead, they prefer to invest in gold, which although it does not pay interest, can maintain or even increase its value over time. On the other hand, when interest rates rise, gold may lose some of its appeal, as investors can get better returns in other assets. However, this is not always so simple, as other factors can counteract this effect.

The currency in which gold is traded also has a major impact on its price. Gold is primarily priced in US dollars, which means that when the dollar strengthens, gold tends to fall in price. This is because when the dollar is stronger, it takes less money to buy the same amount of gold. Conversely, when the dollar weakens, the price of gold rises, because it takes more money to acquire it. This inverse relationship between the dollar and gold is something that traders should keep in mind when analyzing the market.

Another factor that cannot be ignored is speculation. Many traders and investment funds buy and sell gold not necessarily because they need it as a safe haven asset, but to make short-term profits. These speculators often buy gold when they think the price is going to rise and sell it quickly when they feel they have made enough profit. This type of activity can cause large fluctuations in the price of gold, sometimes without a clear economic reason behind it. The behavior of speculators can lead to sudden spikes in the price of gold, which in turn attracts more investors and creates a cycle of high volatility.

Technology also plays a lesser-known role in gold price dynamics. In recent decades, gold has been increasingly used in electronic devices such as mobile phones and computers due to its excellent ability to conduct electricity. Although the amount of gold used in each device is small, the growing global demand for technology has also increased the demand for gold in industry. This means that when the technology industry grows, the demand for gold increases, which can push prices up.

Finally, it is important to mention that the gold market is global, meaning that what happens in one part of the world can affect its price in another. For example, if a crisis or a change in the laws affecting mining occurs in a gold-producing country, this can cause the price of gold to rise worldwide. The same goes for demand: if demand increases in China or India, where gold is highly valued culturally, this can cause prices to rise on international markets.

In short, the price of gold is constantly changing and is influenced by a number of factors, from inflation to central bank decisions, politics and interest rates. Understanding these dynamics allows you to anticipate market movements and take advantage of opportunities as they arise.

Although gold is a stable asset over the long term, fluctuations in its price can offer great opportunities for those who know how to read the right signals and act at the right time.

How to Invest in Physical Gold

Investing in physical gold is one of the most traditional and easiest ways to get into the gold market. Throughout history, people have acquired gold in the form of bullion, coins, or even jewelry to protect their wealth. Today, it remains a popular choice, especially for those who prefer to have something tangible, something they can see and touch. Unlike other forms of investment, such as stocks or bonds, physical gold is an asset that is not dependent on a company or government, and that gives it special value. In this chapter, we will explore how you can invest in physical gold, the different ways to do so, the advantages and disadvantages, and some practical tips to get the most out of this investment.

First, it is important to understand that when we talk about investing in physical gold, we are referring to the purchase of gold bars, gold coins, or in some cases, gold jewelry. Each of these options has its own characteristics and advantages. Gold bars, for example, are pieces of pure gold that come in different sizes and weights. They can be small, such as a gram, or large, such as a kilogram or more. The advantage of bars is that they usually have a lower cost per gram compared to coins or jewelry, making them an ideal option for those looking to maximize their investment.

Gold coins, on the other hand, are another popular way to invest in physical gold. These coins, such as the famous South African Krugerrand or American Eagles, contain a fixed amount of gold and are recognised worldwide. Coins have a special advantage: in addition to the value of the gold they contain, some coins also have a numismatic value. This means that, depending on their rarity and condition, they can be worth more than the gold they contain. However, these types of coins are usually more expensive per gram of gold compared to bullion, as you pay not only for the metal, but also for the design, history and collector demand.

Gold jewelry is perhaps the oldest form of owning physical gold. Throughout history, people have worn gold in the form of rings, necklaces, bracelets, and other adornments. While jewelry can have sentimental and aesthetic value, it is not always the best way to invest in gold. This is because the price of jewelry includes not only the cost of the gold, but also the craftsmanship and design. Additionally, many pieces of jewelry are not made of pure gold, but instead contain a mixture of other metals to make them more durable. For this reason, if your main goal is to invest in gold, bullion or coins are often more cost-effective options.

One of the main advantages of investing in physical gold is that you have something tangible. You can hold it in your hands, store it in a safe, and feel secure in the knowledge that you own an asset that has held its value for thousands of years. No matter what happens in the financial markets or the global economy, your gold will always be there. This sense of security is one of the reasons why many people choose to invest in physical gold instead of opting for more abstract investments like stocks or mutual funds.

However, there are also some disadvantages to consider when investing in physical gold. The first and most obvious is storage. Unlike digital investments, physical gold takes up space and must be stored securely. This may mean having to buy a safe for your home or rent a safe deposit box from a bank. In both cases, there is a cost associated with storing gold that you need to consider. Additionally, there is security to consider. Keeping physical gold at home can be a risk, especially if you don't take steps to protect it.

Another important aspect is that while physical gold is an excellent store of value over the long term, it does not generate any kind of return. Unlike stocks or bonds, which can generate dividends or interest, physical gold simply sits there, waiting for its value to rise over time. This means that while it is a stable investment, it does not offer the same benefits as other types of investments that can generate passive income. However, for many people, this stability and security is more than enough to justify the investment.

When it comes to buying physical gold, it's crucial to make sure you're buying from a reputable seller. The gold market, being so valuable, can attract scammers trying to sell low-quality gold or even counterfeits. That's why it's advisable to do your research before making a purchase and make sure the seller has a good reputation. Additionally, it's always a good idea to ask for certifications proving the authenticity and purity of the gold you're buying. Gold bars and coins often come with these certifications, giving you peace of mind that you're getting what you pay for.

Another thing you need to consider is the price of gold at the time of purchase. The price of gold fluctuates on a daily basis, and while it's always difficult to predict exactly when the best time to buy is, it's a good idea to stay on top of market trends. If you notice that the price of gold has been falling, it may be a good time to buy, while if the price is at a high peak, you might consider waiting a bit for it to drop. Patience is key when it comes to investing in physical gold, as it's often more beneficial to hold it for the long term rather than looking for quick profits.

In short, investing in physical gold is one of the oldest and safest ways to protect your wealth. Whether in the form of bullion, coins, or even jewelry, gold offers a stability that few other investments can match. However, it is important to consider storage costs, security, and the fact that it does not generate returns on its own. If you decide to invest in physical gold, make sure you do so in an informed manner, purchasing through trusted sellers and staying aware of fluctuations in price. With the right strategy, physical gold can be an excellent addition to your long-term investment portfolio.

Trading Gold in the Futures Market

Trading gold in the futures market is one of the most exciting and potentially lucrative ways to invest in this precious metal. Unlike buying physical gold, which involves owning bullion or coins, trading futures allows you to speculate on the price of gold without having to store it. The futures market is ideal for those looking to take advantage of short-term fluctuations in the gold price and who are willing to take on more risk. However, to do it well, it is essential to understand how this type of trading works, what futures contracts are, and what factors affect your success.

First, it's important to understand what a futures contract is. A futures contract is basically an agreement to buy or sell an asset, in this case gold, at a future date at a price agreed upon today. For example, you might sign a contract to buy 100 ounces of gold three months from now for a price set at the time of signing. It doesn't mean you'll actually receive 100 ounces of gold, but rather that you're betting that the price of gold will rise or fall during that time. If the price rises above the value you agreed upon, you can sell your contract before the expiration date and make a profit. If the price falls, you could lose money.

One of the most attractive aspects of the futures market is leverage. When you buy a gold futures contract, you don't have to pay the full value of the gold you're buying. Instead, you only need to deposit a small percentage of the total value, known as "margin." This allows you to control a large amount of gold with a relatively small investment. For example, if the price of gold is $1,800 per ounce and you buy a contract representing 100 ounces, you'd be controlling $180,000 worth of gold. But thanks to leverage, you'd only need to pay a fraction of that, say $10,000. If the price of gold goes up by $10 per ounce, you could make $1,000 on that small initial investment.

Leverage is a double-edged sword. If the price of gold moves in the direction you expected, the gains can be huge. But if the price goes in the opposite direction, the losses can also be significant. This is one of the main risks of trading gold futures. Unlike buying physical gold, where you can simply hold the gold until its value increases, in the futures market you are limited by time. Each contract has an expiration date, and if things don't go as you expected, you could be forced to sell at a loss before the contract expires. That's why trading gold futures is not suitable for everyone; it requires a solid understanding of the market, a clear strategy, and the ability to manage risks.

Another interesting feature of trading gold futures is that you can make money both when the price goes up and when it goes down. If you think the price of gold is going to go up, you can "buy" a futures contract, which is known as "going long." If you are right and the price goes up, you can sell the contract at a higher price and make a profit. But if you think the price of gold is going to go down, you can "sell" a futures contract, which is called "going short." In this case, if the price of gold goes down, you can buy back the contract at a lower price and pocket the difference. This flexibility makes the futures market attractive in both bull and bear markets.

Gold futures trading is also influenced by many of the same factors that affect the price of gold in general. Inflation, interest rates, geopolitics, and the strength of the dollar are all factors that can cause the price of gold to rise or fall. For example, if investors fear that inflation is about to rise, they might start buying gold, which would drive up its price. If the US dollar weakens against other currencies, the price of gold could rise, as more money is needed to buy the same amount of gold. As a trader, it is critical to stay on top of this news and trends in order to make informed decisions.

The futures market is also heavily influenced by large financial players, such as banks, hedge funds, and professional traders. These large participants often have access to advanced information and analysis that can help them anticipate market movements before small investors. This can make the futures market more volatile, with prices moving quickly in response to new information or decisions by these players. For individual traders, this can be an opportunity to make profits if they are alert and quick to react, but it can also be a risk, as sudden market movements can lead to large losses.

Using technical analysis tools is crucial when trading gold futures. Unlike those who buy physical gold for the long term, futures traders often rely on charts and patterns to predict short-term movements in the gold price. Historical price charts, support and resistance levels, and indicators such as moving averages are all tools that can help identify buying or selling opportunities. This technical approach is important because the gold futures market often moves quickly and in short time frames, meaning that decisions must be made based on hard data and not just gut feelings.

It is essential to have a solid risk management strategy when trading gold futures. Leverage and volatility can lead to large gains, but they can also lead to considerable losses. One way to manage this risk is by using "stop-loss" orders, which allow you to limit your losses. For example, if you buy a futures contract and the price of gold starts to fall, a stop-loss order will automatically sell your contract when the price reaches a predetermined level, limiting your losses. Similarly, you can also set "take-profits" to lock in your profits when the price reaches a certain level.

In summary, trading gold in the futures market is an advanced form of investment that can offer great opportunities, but it also carries significant risks. With gold futures, you can take advantage of leverage to control large amounts of gold with a relatively small investment, and you can make money whether the price of gold goes up or down. However, market volatility and leverage risk require careful strategy and a good understanding of how the market works. For those willing to learn and manage these risks, the gold futures market can be a powerful tool for building wealth.

Trading Gold Through ETFs and Funds

Trading gold through ETFs and funds is a popular and accessible way to invest in the gold market without having to buy the physical metal or deal with the complexity of futures. ETFs, or exchange-traded funds, and mutual funds allow you to participate in gold price movements in a simpler and more convenient way. Through these financial instruments, you can gain exposure to gold as an asset without the need to store bullion or coins, and without having to worry about the logistical challenges of investing directly in physical gold. This approach has a number of advantages, such as ease of buying and selling, diversification, and accessibility for all types of investors.

First, it's important to understand what an ETF is. A gold ETF is an exchange-traded fund that tracks the price of gold, meaning its value is tied directly to the price of gold on the market. These funds are typically backed by physical gold, meaning the fund holds actual gold in vaults to back each share of the ETF that is sold to investors. When you buy shares of a gold ETF, you're not buying bullion or coins, but rather you're buying a stake in a fund that owns gold.

This is one of the easiest and most affordable ways to invest in gold, as you can buy and sell shares of the ETF at any time during market hours, just as if you were buying shares of a company.

One of the main advantages of trading gold through ETFs is liquidity. ETFs are traded on stock exchanges, meaning you can easily buy or sell them during market hours. You don't have to worry about finding a buyer or seller, as you might with physical gold, or deal with complicated intermediaries. This allows you to be more flexible in your investment strategy. If you see that the price of gold is rising rapidly, you can buy shares of the ETF at that time. If, on the other hand, you think the price of gold is going to fall, you can sell your shares and exit the investment just as easily.

Another great advantage is that gold ETFs are accessible to almost any investor. Unlike buying physical gold, which can require a significant initial investment, ETFs allow investors to purchase small amounts of gold. You can buy one or multiple shares of an ETF, allowing you to invest according to your financial means. This makes them a great option for both small and large investors. Plus, since ETFs can be purchased through any online brokerage platform, it is very easy to start trading in them.

It is also important to mention that although gold ETFs are backed by physical gold, you do not have to worry about storage or security. The fund takes care of those aspects. This eliminates the additional storage and insurance costs that usually accompany the purchase of physical gold. Also, since ETFs are regulated and regularly audited, you can be sure that the gold backing the fund is actually there. This offers additional peace of mind as you do not have to worry about the authenticity or condition of the gold you indirectly own.

Aside from ETFs, another way to invest in gold is through mutual funds. Unlike ETFs, which are traded like stocks on an exchange, mutual funds are managed by professionals who buy and sell assets on behalf of investors. There are specialized gold mutual funds, which invest in a combination of gold-related assets, such as physical gold, shares of gold mining companies, or even gold futures contracts. The advantage of these funds is that they offer automatic diversification. You are not only investing in the price of gold, but also in other areas of the gold industry, which can reduce risk if the price of gold fluctuates a lot.

Gold mutual funds are typically actively managed, meaning that fund managers make decisions about when to buy or sell assets to try to maximize the fund's profits. This can be beneficial for investors who do not have the time or knowledge to manage their own investment portfolio. However, one disadvantage of mutual funds compared to ETFs is that mutual funds typically have higher fees due to active management. Also, mutual funds are not as liquid as ETFs. If you decide to sell your holdings in a mutual fund, you may have to wait until the end of the day or even several days for the transaction to complete.

One of the common questions investors ask is whether it is better to invest in a gold ETF or a mutual fund. The answer depends on your investment goals and how much control you want to have over your investments. If you prefer flexibility and the ability to buy and sell quickly, ETFs are probably the best option. If, on the other hand, you prefer a more diversified strategy and are comfortable paying higher fees in exchange for professional management, then a mutual fund could be a good alternative. Each option has its advantages, and the important thing is to choose the one that best fits your profile as an investor.

When it comes to choosing a gold ETF, it's important to do your research and compare the options available. There are many gold ETFs on the market, and not all of them are created equal. Some ETFs are backed by physical gold, while others are more focused on futures contracts or shares of gold mining companies. It's also crucial to consider associated costs, such as management fees, as these can impact your long-term returns. It's a good idea to choose an ETF with low fees and a solid track record of tracking the price of gold.

Another important aspect to consider is the risk associated with gold ETFs and funds. Although gold tends to be a relatively stable asset, gold prices can fluctuate in response to global economic events, such as inflation, interest rates, or the strength of the dollar. Also, if you are investing in an ETF or fund that includes shares of gold mining companies, it is important to remember that these stocks are subject to the same risks as any other company on the stock market, such as poor management or low productivity. Therefore, it is important to keep in mind that although gold ETFs and funds are less risky than trading futures, they are still not risk-free.

In conclusion, trading gold through ETFs and funds is an accessible, flexible and effective way to invest in this valuable asset. ETFs allow you to benefit from gold price increases without having to worry about storage and security, while mutual funds offer you a diversified and professionally managed option. Both alternatives are ideal for those who want exposure to the gold market without the logistical challenges of owning physical gold or the complexity of futures contracts. As always, it is essential to do your research before investing and ensure that the option chosen is suited to your goals and risk profile.

Gold Trading in the Forex Market

Gold trading on the Forex market is one of the most interesting and versatile ways to trade this precious metal. Unlike buying physical gold or trading futures contracts, Forex allows you to speculate on the value of gold against different currencies, usually the US dollar (USD). This means that you are not only betting on changes in the price of gold, but also on the relationship between gold and currencies. This type of trading offers great flexibility, leverage, and the possibility of profiting in both bullish and bearish markets. However, it also involves risks that are important to understand before diving into this world.

First, it is critical to understand how the Forex market works and how gold is traded on it. Forex, or the foreign exchange market, is the world's largest financial market, where currencies are traded 24 hours a day, 5 days a week. In this market, gold is treated as a "currency" that is primarily traded against the US dollar, under the symbol XAU/USD. This means that instead of buying or selling gold directly, what you are doing is trading the value of gold in terms of dollars. If you think the price of gold will rise relative to the dollar, you buy XAU/USD. If you think the price of gold will fall, you sell XAU/USD. This process is similar to trading any currency pair on Forex.

One of the key advantages of trading gold on the Forex market is the ability to profit from both rising and falling price movements. In a bull market, when you expect the price of gold to rise, you can open a buy position (also known as going long). If the price of gold does indeed rise, you can close your position at a higher price and make a profit. But the interesting thing about Forex is that you can also open a sell position (go short) if you think the price of gold is going to fall. In this case, you would sell gold at a high price and when the price falls, you would buy it back at a lower price, making the difference as profit.

Leverage is another important feature of the Forex market. Leverage allows you to control a much larger amount of gold with a relatively small initial investment. For example, if you trade with 1:100 leverage, you can control 100 times the value of your investment. This means that if you invest $1,000, you could be controlling $100,000 worth of gold. Leverage can amplify your gains if the price of gold moves in your favor, but it can also amplify your losses if the market goes against your position. For this reason, it is critical to use leverage prudently and manage risk well to avoid significant losses.

One aspect that makes gold a popular asset in Forex is its role as a safe haven. In times of economic uncertainty, geopolitical crises, or recessions, many investors turn to gold to protect their capital, which can cause the price of gold to rise. This creates interesting trading opportunities, as the price of gold tends to rise when stock markets fall or when currencies such as the dollar lose value. This makes gold an excellent choice for traders looking to take advantage of times of volatility in the financial markets. If you know how to interpret the right signals, such as changes in economic policies or important global events, you can identify when is the best time to buy or sell gold in Forex.

Gold is also closely correlated to the US dollar, meaning that the value of gold in the Forex market can be influenced by the strength or weakness of the dollar. If the dollar weakens against other currencies, the price of gold generally tends to rise, as more dollars are needed to buy the same amount of gold. On the other hand, if the dollar strengthens, the price of gold can fall. This creates opportunities for traders who monitor fluctuations in the Forex market and understand how the value of the dollar can impact the price of gold. In addition, Federal Reserve policies, such as interest rate changes or economic stimulus measures, can also have a significant effect on the price of gold, adding another level of complexity and opportunity to Forex gold trading.

Technical analysis is a key tool for successful gold trading in the Forex market. Traders in this market often use price charts and a variety of technical indicators to identify patterns and trends that help them predict where the price of gold will move. Support and resistance levels, moving averages, the Relative Strength Index (RSI), and Bollinger Bands are some of the most common indicators traders use to analyze gold price action. This type of analysis is especially useful in Forex, where prices can move quickly in response to news or economic events.

In addition to technical analysis, fundamental analysis also plays an important role in Forex gold trading. This involves being aware of economic and political factors that can affect the price of gold. Interest rates, inflation levels, global supply and demand for gold, and geopolitical tensions are just some of the factors that can move the gold market. For example, if a major gold-producing country experiences a political crisis that affects its ability to mine and export gold, this could reduce global supply and cause the price of gold to rise. Similarly, if central banks of major countries decide to increase their gold reserves, this could also drive up prices. Staying informed about these factors can give you a significant advantage when trading gold on Forex.

Another benefit of trading gold on Forex is that you can access the market 24 hours a day. The Forex market never closes during business days, meaning you can trade gold at any time that is convenient for you, whether it is overnight or in the morning hours. This is especially useful for those traders who have limited hours or who prefer to trade in different market sessions, such as the Asian, European, or American sessions. The ability to trade gold at any time gives you more flexibility to take advantage of opportunities when they arise, and you are not restricted by the market hours of other financial instruments.

However, like any form of trading, trading gold on the Forex market is not without risk. Rapid fluctuations in the price of gold can result in large gains or losses in a short period of time. That's why it's crucial to have a clear strategy and know how to manage risk effectively. This includes setting stop-loss levels to limit your losses in case the market moves against you and not risking more money than you're willing to lose. Discipline is key in Forex, especially when trading an asset as volatile as gold.

In short, trading gold on the Forex market is a dynamic and flexible way to invest in this precious metal. It offers you the opportunity to speculate on gold price movements in relation to the US dollar, and to profit in both bullish and bearish markets. With the proper use of leverage, technical and fundamental analysis, and prudent risk management, trading gold on the Forex can be a powerful tool for generating income. However, due to the volatility and associated risks, it is essential that you prepare well, do thorough research, and trade responsibly to maximize your chances of success.

The Role of Gold in a Diversified Portfolio

The role of gold in a diversified portfolio is a topic of great importance to any investor looking to protect their wealth while maximising their long-term growth opportunities. Throughout history, gold has been considered a safe haven, a refuge in times of crisis and an effective tool for balancing an investment portfolio. But what exactly does it mean to diversify a portfolio? Diversifying involves spreading your investments across a variety of different assets to reduce risk. And this is where gold comes in, as it has unique characteristics that make it valuable for any diversification strategy.

First, it is important to understand why gold is considered a safe haven. Over the centuries, gold has been valued for its ability to maintain its value in times of economic, political or social uncertainty. When stock markets fall, or when economies face recessions, gold tends to behave in the opposite way, rising in value or at least remaining stable. This is because investors view gold as a reliable store of value in difficult times. Therefore, including gold in a diversified portfolio can help reduce overall volatility, as its performance is not directly tied to the ups and downs of the stock market.

A clear example of this occurred during the 2008 global financial crisis. As stock markets around the world plummeted and many assets lost value, the price of gold rose significantly. Investors who held gold in their portfolios saw how this asset helped cushion losses from other investments. This is one of the key benefits of having gold in a diversified portfolio – its ability to act as a buffer during times of high volatility. Even if the rest of your portfolio is suffering, gold can maintain its value or even increase, giving you an extra layer of protection.

Another reason why gold is useful in a diversified portfolio is its low correlation with other financial assets. In simple terms, assets that are correlated tend to move in the same direction. For example, if you have several stocks in your portfolio and the stock market falls, chances are that most of those stocks will lose value at the same time. However, gold tends to have a negative or low correlation with traditional assets, such as stocks and bonds.

This means that when the stock market falls, gold often moves in the opposite direction or is not affected in the same way. Including an asset like gold in your portfolio helps prevent all of your investments from behaving the same way in times of crisis, thereby reducing overall risk.

In addition to its role as a safe haven and low-correlation asset, gold is also a good hedge against inflation. Inflation occurs when the prices of goods and services rise, reducing the purchasing power of money. During times of high inflation, traditional assets such as stocks or bonds can lose value as the money you earn from them is worth less. However, gold tends to increase in value during periods of inflation. This is because gold is a finite resource – it cannot be easily printed or created like money. As inflation increases, demand for gold typically grows because investors see it as a way to protect their purchasing power. Therefore, having gold in a diversified portfolio can help protect you against the impact of inflation.

Another interesting aspect of gold is that it is a tangible asset. Unlike stocks, bonds, or cryptocurrencies, which are intangible assets that you cannot see or touch, gold is a physical asset. This physical aspect of gold makes it attractive to many investors who want to own something that has intrinsic value. For centuries, gold has been used as currency and as a symbol of wealth and stability. Although we do not use gold directly as money today, its value is still recognized around the world. Having physical gold in a portfolio provides a sense of security that cannot be obtained with other types of financial assets.

Now, it is important to mention that although gold has many benefits, it is not advisable to have your entire portfolio invested in gold. Although it is a valuable asset for diversification, it also has its drawbacks. For example, gold does not generate passive income like bonds or stocks do. When you invest in bonds, you receive interest payments, and when you invest in stocks, you may receive dividends. However, gold does not generate any type of income on its own. It simply benefits you if its price goes up and you can sell it at a higher price. For this reason, gold should be viewed as a component of your portfolio, not the only investment.

As for how much gold you should have in your portfolio, that depends on your financial goals, risk tolerance, and investment horizon. Some experts recommend that gold make up 5% to 10% of a well-diversified portfolio. This amount can vary depending on market conditions. If the stock market is particularly volatile, or if inflation is rising rapidly, you might consider increasing your exposure to gold. On the other hand, in times of economic stability, you may prefer to keep a smaller portion of your portfolio in gold.

In addition to physical gold, you can also diversify your portfolio by investing in other gold-related assets, such as shares of gold mining companies, gold ETFs, or mutual funds that invest in gold. Shares of gold mining companies can offer higher returns than physical gold if gold prices rise, but they also carry more risk, as the value of these shares can be affected by factors outside of gold prices, such as company management or mine productivity. Gold ETFs and mutual funds are a simpler and less risky option, as they allow you to invest in a wide range of gold-related assets without having to worry about the details of each individual investment.

Finally, it is important to remember that diversification is not just about investing in gold, but about building a balanced portfolio that includes a variety of assets that behave differently in various market conditions. Gold can act as an excellent hedge and offer stability in times of uncertainty, but it is also essential to include other assets, such as stocks, bonds and real estate, to ensure solid growth over the long term. The key to investment success is to have a diversified strategy that allows you to profit in both good and bad times.

In conclusion, gold plays a critical role in a diversified portfolio due to its ability to protect against volatility, its low correlation with other assets, its value as a safe haven, and its ability to mitigate the impact of inflation. Although it does not generate passive income and may not be suitable as a sole investment, gold does offer intrinsic value that can protect your wealth in times of economic uncertainty. Incorporating gold into your investment strategy is an effective way to ensure that your portfolio is prepared for any eventuality that the financial markets may face.

Technical Analysis for Gold Trading

Technical analysis is one of the most important and powerful tools that traders use to make decisions in the gold market. Unlike fundamental analysis, which focuses on economic factors and global news that can influence the price of gold, technical analysis is based on the study of price charts. In simple terms, it involves looking at past movements in the price of gold to try to predict its future behavior. The idea behind technical analysis is that the price of an asset already reflects all relevant information and that historical patterns tend to repeat themselves over time. This makes it a key tool for any trader looking to take advantage of opportunities in the gold market.

The first step in using technical analysis in gold trading is to become familiar with price charts. Charts show the evolution of the gold price over time and can be set to display different time frames, from minutes to years. Japanese candlestick charts are the most commonly used by traders, as they provide a wealth of information at a glance. Each candle on the chart represents a time period, such as an hour, day, or week, and displays four key pieces of information: the opening price, the closing price, the highest price, and the lowest price in that period. If the candle is light-colored, it means that the closing price was higher than the opening price (a bullish signal), while a dark-colored candle indicates that the closing price was lower than the opening price (a bearish signal). These charts help traders visualize market behavior and identify patterns.

One of the most basic and widely used concepts in technical analysis is that of support and resistance. A support level is a price on the chart where gold has tended to stop falling in the past. It is like a "floor" that stops the price from falling beyond a certain point. On the other hand, a resistance level is a price where gold has had difficulty rising further, acting as a "ceiling" that stops the price from advancing. Traders look for these key levels because they are often points where the price of gold can change direction. For example, if the price of gold is near a support level, a trader may decide to buy, hoping that the price will bounce back up. Likewise, if the price is approaching a resistance level, it could be an opportunity to sell, as there is a high probability that the price will fall.

In addition to support and resistance levels, traders also use tools such as moving averages to analyze gold price trends. A moving average is simply the average of the gold price over a specific time period, and it can be used to smooth out daily fluctuations and make trends easier to identify. Moving averages can be short-, medium-, or long-term, and traders often look at how they interact with each other to look for buy or sell signals. For example, if a short-term moving average crosses above a long-term moving average, this can be a sign that the gold price is entering an uptrend. Likewise, if the short-term moving average crosses below the long-term moving average, it can be a sign that the price is entering a downtrend.

Another popular technical indicator is the Relative Strength Index (RSI). The RSI is an indicator that measures the speed and change of gold price movements to determine whether the market is overbought or oversold. The RSI is expressed in a range from 0 to 100. If the RSI is above 70, this may indicate that gold is overbought, meaning that the price has risen too quickly and a correction is likely soon. Conversely, if the RSI is below 30, this suggests that gold is oversold and there could be a buying opportunity as the price may bounce back up. This indicator is useful because it helps traders identify when a move in the gold price has gone too far and could reverse.

Bollinger bands are another indicator that traders commonly use for technical analysis of gold. This indicator consists of three lines: a moving average in the middle and two bands above and below this average. Bollinger bands expand and contract based on market volatility. When the bands are far apart, it indicates that the market is more volatile; when they are closer together, the market is less volatile. Traders look at how the price of gold interacts with these bands to make trading decisions. If the price touches or breaks the upper band, it may be a sign that gold is overbought and the price could pull back. If the price touches or breaks the lower band, it could be a sign that gold is oversold and the price could bounce back.

An important aspect of technical analysis is identifying chart patterns. Patterns are specific formations that the gold price creates on a chart that can signal a change in market direction. Some of the most common patterns include the "head-and-shoulders," which is a reversal pattern that often indicates that an uptrend is about to change to a downtrend. Another common pattern is the "triangle," which can signal a consolidation in price before the market decides which direction to move. Traders who are skilled at identifying these patterns can use them to anticipate movements in the gold price and make more informed trading decisions.

Technical analysis also takes into account trading volumes, which are a measure of how many contracts or units of gold are being bought and sold at any given time. Volumes can offer clues about the strength of a trend. For example, if the price of gold is rising but volumes are low, this could indicate that the uptrend is not very strong and could soon reverse. Conversely, if the price is rising and volumes are also high, this suggests that the trend has a solid foundation and is likely to continue. Volume analysis can be especially useful when used in conjunction with other technical indicators to confirm buy or sell signals.

While technical analysis is a valuable tool, it is important to remember that it is not infallible. No indicator or pattern can predict the future with certainty, and there is always a risk that the market will move in an unexpected direction. For this reason, traders often combine technical analysis with other strategies, such as fundamental analysis or risk management, to increase their chances of success. Furthermore, technical analysis requires practice and patience. It is not enough to simply learn how to identify indicators; it is also crucial to know how to interpret them in the proper context and make trading decisions based on careful analysis rather than emotional impulses.

Finally, it is important to mention that technical analysis is most effective when applied in a consistent and disciplined manner. Successful traders do not rely solely on one signal or indicator; instead, they look for confirmation from multiple sources before making a decision. For example, if a trader sees that the gold price is near a support level, they may wait for the RSI to indicate that gold is oversold before buying. Likewise, if the gold price breaks a resistance level, the trader may wait for the Bollinger Bands to widen to confirm that the uptrend is strong. This methodical, confirmation-based approach is what distinguishes successful traders from those who act impulsively.

In short, technical analysis is a fundamental tool for gold trading, as it allows traders to make informed decisions based on the study of price movements and historical patterns. By using charts, technical indicators such as the RSI, Bollinger Bands, and support and resistance analysis, traders can identify buying and selling opportunities and manage their trades more effectively. However, technical analysis is not a guarantee of success, and should always be combined with a solid risk management strategy and a disciplined mindset. With practice and time, technical analysis can become an essential part of your arsenal as a gold trader.

Fundamental Analysis of the Gold Market

Fundamental analysis is an essential tool for understanding the gold market and making informed decisions about when to buy or sell this valuable metal. Unlike technical analysis, which relies on the study of charts and price patterns, fundamental analysis focuses on the economic, political, and social factors that can influence the value of gold. In other words, it's about looking at what's happening in the world and how those events can affect the supply and demand for gold, which, in turn, impacts its price. Understanding these factors can help you make more strategic and less impulsive decisions when trading gold.

One of the main factors influencing the price of gold is the monetary policy of central banks, especially the US central bank, the Federal Reserve (Fed). The Fed has the power to influence interest rates and the amount of money in circulation, which can have a direct impact on the price of gold. For example, when the Fed raises interest rates, gold tends to fall in price. This happens because higher interest rates make bonds and other financial assets more attractive to investors, which reduces the demand for gold. Conversely, when the Fed lowers interest rates, gold typically rises in price as investors seek safe havens like gold instead of assets offering lower returns.

In addition to monetary policy, inflation is another key factor affecting the gold market. Inflation occurs when the prices of goods and services rise, which reduces the value of money. During periods of high inflation, investors tend to look for assets that protect their purchasing power, and gold has proven to be one of the best ways to do so. Gold is considered a store of value because, over time, it has maintained its value even when currencies have lost theirs. For example, if prices in general rise due to inflation, the value of gold also tends to rise, as more people try to buy it to protect themselves against the loss of value of their money. In this way, gold acts as a safe haven during times of economic uncertainty.

Fiscal policy and government debt also play a major role in the price of gold. When governments increase government spending or incur high levels of debt, investors often become concerned about future economic stability. This uncertainty can lead to an increase in demand for gold as investors seek to protect themselves against potential economic crises or currency depreciation. In times of high government debt or when a country appears to be printing more money than it should, gold becomes an attractive option for investors who wish to take refuge in an asset that has historically been considered safe.

Another factor that influences the price of gold is the demand for physical gold, especially in countries like China and India, which are some of the largest consumers of gold in the world. In these countries, gold is not only seen as an investment, but also as a status symbol and a culturally important commodity, especially at events like weddings and festivals. When the demand for gold increases in these countries, the global price of the metal tends to rise. For example, in India, during the wedding season, the demand for gold often skyrockets, leading to an increase in international prices. Similarly, when the economy of these countries grows, the demand for gold increases, which can cause prices to rise even further.

In addition to the demand for gold in jewelry, there is also a high demand for gold from institutional investors and central banks. Central banks around the world hold large reserves of gold as a way to diversify their assets and protect themselves against the devaluation of their currencies. When central banks buy gold, the price usually rises due to increased demand. On the other hand, if central banks decide to sell part of their gold reserves, the price can fall. This interaction between global supply and demand is a key component of fundamental gold analysis.

Another key aspect that affects the gold market is geopolitical events. In times of international tensions, armed conflicts or political crises, gold tends to rise in price. This is because gold is seen as a safe haven in times of uncertainty. When financial markets are volatile due to geopolitical instability, investors look for assets that offer them security, and gold has historically fulfilled that role. A clear example of this occurred in 2011, when economic and political instability in various parts of the world led to a significant increase in the price of gold, reaching historic highs.

The value of the US dollar also has a direct impact on the price of gold. Since gold is primarily priced in dollars on international markets, any change in the value of the dollar can affect its price. When the dollar strengthens, gold tends to fall in price as it becomes more expensive for investors who buy gold with other currencies. Conversely, when the dollar weakens, gold tends to rise in price as it becomes more accessible to foreign investors. This is an important aspect for gold traders to keep in mind as movements in the value of the dollar can significantly influence the gold market.

Gold supply and production also play a role in its price. Gold is a finite resource, meaning its supply is limited. Gold mining is an expensive and complex process, and the amount of gold that can be extracted from the ground is decreasing over time. As gold mines become less productive and more difficult to operate, the cost of mining gold increases, which can lead to an increase in prices. Additionally, if major gold-producing regions, such as South Africa, Australia, or Russia, face political, economic, or environmental problems that affect gold production, the global supply of gold may decrease, which would also drive prices higher.

An often overlooked aspect of fundamental gold analysis is the impact of technology. Although gold is traditionally used in jewelry and as an investment, it also has technological applications, especially in electronics and medicine. As technology advances and demand for gold in these sectors grows, its price can be affected. For example, gold is used in the manufacture of electronic components due to its high conductivity and resistance to corrosion. If demand for electronic devices increases, so will the demand for gold in this sector, which could have a positive impact on its price.

In summary, fundamental analysis of the gold market involves examining a wide range of economic, political and social factors that can influence its price. Among the most important are central bank monetary policies, inflation, demand for physical gold in key countries such as China and India, geopolitical events, the value of the dollar, the global supply of gold and technological demand. By understanding how these factors affect the supply and demand for gold, investors and traders can make more informed and strategic decisions about when to buy or sell gold. Although fundamental analysis cannot accurately predict future movements in the price of gold, it does provide a solid basis for making decisions based on economic and global reality, rather than relying solely on charts and patterns. Fundamental analysis is therefore an essential tool for anyone who wants to trade the gold market successfully and for the long term.

The Impact of Central Banks on the Price of Gold

The impact of central banks on the price of gold is one of the most important topics that any trader or investor should understand. Central banks are not only the institutions in charge of managing countries' monetary policies, but they also play a key role in the buying and selling of gold, which directly affects its price. Central banks, such as the US Federal Reserve, the European Central Bank, or the People's Bank of China, hold large reserves of gold and often buy and sell the metal as part of their strategy to manage their economies. These actions can have a significant effect on the global gold market.

One of the main roles of central banks is to manage their countries' monetary policy, which includes setting interest rates. Interest rates are critical to the value of gold, as they influence the profitability of other investments, such as bonds. When central banks raise interest rates, investors tend to move their money into yield-earning assets, such as government bonds, rather than holding them in gold, which does not pay interest or dividends. This can cause demand for gold to decrease, leading to a fall in its price. On the other hand, when central banks lower interest rates, gold becomes more attractive, as investors look for safe assets that are not dependent on interest rates. This often results in an increase in demand for gold, and therefore its price.

Money supply management is also a key factor in central banks' influence over gold. When central banks inject large amounts of money into the economy through policies such as quantitative easing, this tends to devalue the local currency. When a country's currency weakens, gold becomes more attractive as a store of value, as it is not tied to any particular currency. This can cause the price of gold to rise, as more people and countries seek to protect themselves against the loss of value of their money by buying gold. Conversely, when a central bank restricts the money supply or strengthens its currency, gold can become less attractive, putting downward pressure on its price.

Gold reserves held by central banks also play an important role in the gold market. For many years, central banks have held large amounts of gold as part of their international reserves. These reserves are not only a sign of economic stability, but also act as a backing for the country's currency. However, the amount of gold that central banks decide to buy or sell can have a major impact on global prices. If a central bank of a major country decides to significantly increase its gold reserves, this can cause an increase in demand and a rise in prices. On the other hand, if central banks decide to sell large amounts of gold, the price can fall due to the increase in the supply available on the market.

One of the clearest examples of how central banks affect the price of gold is what happened during the financial crisis of 2008. At that time, central banks around the world adopted expansionary monetary policies to combat the crisis, which included lowering interest rates and massively injecting money into economies. As a result of these actions, many people and countries lost confidence in the financial system and sought refuge in gold. This caused the price of gold to skyrocket to record levels, as more and more investors bought the metal as a way to protect themselves against economic instability.

Another area where central banks have a significant impact on the price of gold is through their decisions to buy or sell gold on international markets. When a large central bank, such as that of China or Russia, decides to increase its gold reserves, this can have an immediate effect on the global price of gold. These central banks often buy large amounts of gold in one go, which increases demand and drives up prices. Similarly, if they decide to sell part of their reserves, this can cause the price to fall due to increased supply in the market. This is why traders and analysts often keep an eye on the policies and actions of central banks, as their decisions can create significant opportunities or risks in the gold market.

An interesting aspect of the relationship between central banks and gold is that although many countries no longer use the gold standard (a system in which currencies were backed by gold), the metal remains an important part of international reserves. Even in a modern monetary system, where currencies are no longer directly linked to gold, central banks hold gold as a way to diversify their assets and protect themselves against volatility in financial markets. In times of crisis, gold is still considered a safe asset, and central banks often turn to it as a way to ensure economic stability.

Another reason why central banks have such a strong impact on the price of gold is because their monetary policy decisions can lead to inflation or deflation, which in turn affects the value of gold. During times of high inflation, gold typically rises in price, as investors see it as a hedge against currencies losing purchasing power. For example, if a central bank prints too much money or cuts interest rates too much, this can cause prices for goods and services to rise, leading to increased demand for gold as a safe haven. During times of deflation, when prices fall and the value of money rises, the price of gold can fall, as investors prefer to hold cash or other yield-earning assets.

It is also important to understand that central banks do not act in isolation. The policies of one central bank can affect other countries and their respective decisions regarding gold. For example, if the US Federal Reserve raises interest rates, this can lead other central banks to do the same to protect the value of their currencies against the dollar. These coordinated moves can influence the demand for gold globally, causing prices to rise or fall depending on the policies adopted.

In recent years, there has been a growing interest in gold from central banks in emerging economies such as China and Russia. These countries have been purchasing large amounts of gold to diversify their reserves and reduce their dependence on the US dollar. This change in policy by the central banks of these nations has had a significant impact on the gold market, as it has increased global demand and driven prices higher. This is a clear example of how central bank decisions can directly affect the value of gold in international markets.

In short, the impact of central banks on the price of gold is undeniable and manifests itself in a variety of ways. From setting interest rates to managing gold reserves, central banks have the power to influence the supply and demand of this valuable metal. Their monetary policies, decisions on buying and selling gold, and their management of inflation and money supply can cause significant fluctuations in the price of gold, making them a key player in this market. For any trader or investor looking to trade in the gold market, it is essential to closely follow the actions of central banks and understand how their decisions can affect the value of the metal.

Gold Trading During Economic Crises

Gold trading during economic crises is a topic that always generates a lot of interest, as gold has historically been considered a safe haven in times of uncertainty. When economies begin to falter, whether due to a recession, financial crisis or geopolitical issues, many people, from large investors to small savers, turn to gold as a way to protect their money. But why does this happen and how can gold be put to good use during an economic crisis?

During an economic crisis, confidence in traditional financial markets tends to decline. Stock prices fall, currencies may lose value, and bonds, which are usually a safe investment option, may not offer attractive returns. In this context, gold stands out as a solid investment because, unlike stocks or bonds, its value does not depend on a company's profits or a government's policies. Gold is a tangible asset that has been valuable for thousands of years and is still perceived as a hedge against market volatility.

One of the main reasons why gold becomes so attractive in times of crisis is because its price tends to rise when other assets fall. This makes it a safe haven for investors looking to protect their wealth. Throughout history, we have seen this behavior on several occasions. For example, during the 2008 financial crisis, when stock markets collapsed and banking institutions were on the verge of collapse, the price of gold rose considerably. Investors saw it as a way to protect themselves from the chaos that was taking place in the financial markets.

The value of gold during a crisis is also influenced by the perception that it is an inflation-resistant asset. When central banks and governments try to combat an economic crisis, they often adopt policies that inject large amounts of money into the economy, which can lead to high inflation. When money loses value, people look for assets that retain their purchasing power, and gold has proven to be an excellent choice for this. As inflation increases, the price of gold typically rises, offering investors a way to protect themselves from the erosion of the value of their money.

Another reason why gold is valued during economic crises is its independence from financial systems. Unlike stocks or bonds, gold is not dependent on a particular institution or government. It cannot be frozen or controlled by third parties, making it a safe way to store wealth, especially when there is uncertainty about the future of financial institutions. In a crisis, when banks may face difficulties, physical gold remains a safe and tangible asset, something that many investors value highly in times of economic insecurity.

Gold is also seen as a hedge against currency depreciation. During an economic crisis, the currencies of affected countries often lose value, which can lead to instability in foreign exchange markets. If a currency depreciates significantly, gold tends to increase in value in that currency, as it is seen as a more stable alternative. This is especially true in countries where economic crises are more severe, and people prefer to exchange their local currency for gold to prevent their savings from losing value.

Furthermore, gold is an asset that is not dependent on economic cycles in the same way as other financial assets. While stocks often fall in a recession due to declining corporate profits, gold can maintain or even increase its value since it is not dependent on corporate earnings or economic growth. This makes it an attractive option for investors who want to reduce risk in their portfolios during a crisis.

Although gold is generally a solid investment during crises, it is not immune to volatility. Although its price tends to rise in times of uncertainty, it can also experience short-term fluctuations. For example, during a crisis, investors may be forced to sell gold to cover other losses or pay off debts, which can cause the price to temporarily fall. However, over the long term, gold often recovers and continues its upward trend, especially if the crisis persists.

Another important aspect of trading gold during an economic crisis is access to the different markets where gold is traded. During difficult times, investors may choose to buy physical gold, such as bullion or coins, which they can store and own directly. Physical gold is valued for its tangibility, but it has disadvantages, such as storage and security costs. On the other hand, many traders prefer to trade gold derivatives, such as futures or contracts for difference (CFDs), which allow them to profit from fluctuations in the gold price without having to physically own the metal. These financial instruments allow for greater flexibility, especially in times of crisis, when access to physical gold may be limited or expensive.

In addition to traditional options such as futures and ETFs, many traders also turn to the gold markets on Forex. In this market, currency pairs are traded that include gold as a key component. This type of trading is attractive to investors looking to take advantage of both the volatility of gold and fluctuations in exchange rates. During an economic crisis, when currencies can be particularly volatile, gold tends to act as a stabilizer, allowing Forex traders to hedge their positions with gold and profit from its price movements.

One of the biggest challenges of trading gold during an economic crisis is timing. While gold tends to rise in times of uncertainty, it is not always easy to predict when that rise will begin. Sometimes, gold prices can remain stable or even fall during the early stages of a crisis, only to rise again when the situation worsens. That is why it is important to be well informed and closely follow market signals before making hasty decisions. Economic news, central bank decisions and geopolitical events can be key indicators of when there might be a surge in demand for gold.

Finally, it is critical to remember that while gold can be an excellent hedge in times of crisis, it should not be the only investment in a diversified portfolio. It is important to combine gold with other assets, such as bonds and stocks from more crisis-resistant sectors, to maximize profit opportunities and minimize risks. Gold can be an important piece of the puzzle, but it should not be the only option. By having a balanced strategy, investors can better navigate the turbulent waters of an economic crisis and emerge in a stronger position.

In summary, trading gold during economic crises offers great opportunities, but also presents challenges. Gold is a safe haven that investors seek out in times of uncertainty, and its price tends to rise when other assets fall. However, it is critical to understand market dynamics and be prepared for the volatility that can arise in the short term. Leveraging gold as part of a broader, well-diversified strategy can be the key to protecting and growing wealth during difficult times.

The Effect of Geopolitics on the Gold Market

Madelyn Price

The effect of geopolitics on the gold market is a fascinating topic because it combines two seemingly different worlds: international politics and the precious metals market. However, the two are deeply connected. Tensions between countries, wars, trade conflicts, and even a nation's internal political decisions can significantly influence the price of gold. This is because gold, as a safe haven asset, tends to be perceived as a safe investment in times of political or economic uncertainty.

For starters, gold is considered a safe haven because, throughout history, it has maintained its value amidst critical situations. When geopolitical events occur that threaten the stability of a country or the global economic system, investors often turn to gold. This is because, unlike stocks or currencies, gold is not directly tied to a company's performance or a government's monetary policy. Gold is tangible, and its value tends to increase in times of crisis, making it a very valuable asset when things become unpredictable.

One of the most obvious effects of geopolitics on the gold market is the increase in demand for gold during military conflicts. Wars, or even the threat of war, create uncertainty and fear in financial markets. When investors do not know what will happen to economies affected by conflict, they tend to seek safe havens to protect their capital. This is especially true when the war involves major world powers or key regions for the global economy. In such cases, gold becomes a logical choice, as its value is not directly tied to the performance of any particular country.

Take the 2003 invasion of Iraq or the nuclear tensions between North Korea and the United States. In both cases, political and military instability caused the price of gold to soar as investors sought to protect their assets against the possibility of a prolonged war or an economic crisis resulting from the conflict. This pattern has been repeated throughout history: wars often drive the price of gold to higher levels due to investors' search for safety.

In addition to wars, geopolitical tensions such as trade disputes or economic sanctions can also affect the price of gold. In recent years, we have seen how disputes between the United States and China, the two largest economies in the world, have had a direct impact on financial markets, including the gold market. Trade tensions between the two countries have created uncertainty in the markets, and this uncertainty has led to an increase in demand for gold. Investors fear that a prolonged trade war could negatively affect the global economy, and therefore, they seek refuge in assets that are not as exposed to such conflicts.

A clear example is the trade war between the United States and China that began in 2018. As tensions rose and trade tariffs increased, investors began to worry about the impact of this situation on the global economy. This led to an increase in demand for gold, which led to an increase in its price. Investors viewed gold as a hedge against the potential economic slowdown that could arise as a result of the trade dispute. Even as governments attempted to resolve the conflict, uncertainty persisted, keeping interest in gold at high levels.

Another interesting aspect of the effect of geopolitics on the gold market is how economic sanctions and financial restrictions can increase demand for the precious metal. When a country faces international sanctions, as has been the case with Iran or Russia, its access to the global financial system is limited. This can lead to governments and citizens in those countries looking for alternatives to protect their wealth, and one of those alternatives is gold. Throughout history, many sanctioned countries have turned to gold to avoid restrictions placed on their currencies or financial transactions. This not only increases the demand for gold in those countries, but can also affect global prices.

Gold is especially attractive in these scenarios because it is a physical asset that can be stored and transferred without relying on international banking systems. In a context of sanctions or financial restrictions, gold becomes a universal currency that allows governments and individuals to maintain their purchasing power. This is especially important in countries facing severe sanctions, as access to foreign currencies, such as the dollar or euro, may be limited. Gold, on the other hand, remains accessible, making it a key tool to circumvent financial barriers imposed by other governments.

In addition to military conflicts and sanctions, internal political changes in countries can also affect the gold market. Elections, especially in large or influential economies, often create uncertainty about future economic policies. If a key country such as the United States, Germany or China elects a new government with drastically different economic policies, investors may feel uncertain about the future of financial markets. This uncertainty can lead to an increase in demand for gold as a hedge against possible drastic changes in the economy.

A recent example is the election of Donald Trump as President of the United States in 2016. His victory surprised many investors, and uncertainty about the policies he would implement led to a surge in demand for gold in the days following his election. Many feared that his trade and economic policies could destabilize global markets, causing investors to seek safety in gold. Although the stock market eventually recovered and experienced a period of growth, the initial surge in the price of gold showed how political uncertainty can influence metal prices.

Another interesting case is Brexit, the United Kingdom's decision to leave the European Union. From the referendum in 2016 to the country's actual exit in 2020, gold experienced high demand due to the economic and political uncertainty surrounding the separation. Investors did not know how Brexit would affect the UK or EU economy, so many chose to invest in gold as a way to protect themselves against any potential negative impact.

It is important to note that gold does not always rise during all geopolitical events. Sometimes the effects can be temporary or depend on how tensions evolve. For example, if a military conflict is resolved quickly or if a domestic political crisis stabilises, the price of gold can return to lower levels as uncertainty subsides. This means that while geopolitics can have a major impact on the gold market, other factors such as monetary policy and the global economy also need to be taken into account to fully understand price movements.

In summary, geopolitics plays a crucial role in the gold market. Wars, trade tensions, economic sanctions, and internal political changes can all increase demand for gold as investors seek a safe haven in uncertain times. Gold has proven to be a valuable investment in these contexts, offering stability and protection against market fluctuations. However, it is important to remember that the effects of geopolitics on gold are not always predictable or permanent, and traders must keep an eye on other economic factors to make informed decisions.

Gold Trading Secrets for Success

Gold trading can be one of the most exciting and lucrative ways to invest, but it can also be tricky if you don't have the right strategy. Over the years, many traders have tried to find the "secrets" to success in this market. While there is no magic formula that guarantees profits, there are certain principles and strategies that can significantly increase your chances of success. Below, we'll explore some of the secrets of gold trading that can help you become a more efficient and profitable trader.

One of the most important secrets of gold trading is to understand that this precious metal does not behave like other assets. While stocks and currencies are influenced by corporate earnings or the monetary policy of governments, the price of gold is more closely related to macroeconomic and geopolitical factors. For example, when there is uncertainty in the world, such as financial crises or political tensions, gold tends to increase in value. This is because gold is seen as a safe haven, an asset that does not lose value easily in difficult times. Therefore, one of the first secrets to succeeding in gold trading is to pay attention to what is happening on the global scene, as larger events can have a significant impact on gold prices.

Another of the key secrets to gold trading is mastering technical analysis. While fundamental analysis, which assesses economic conditions, is important, technical analysis is essential for determining when to enter and exit a trade. This involves studying price charts and looking for patterns that indicate where the market will go. For example, one of the most common patterns is "support and resistance." Support is a level on the chart where the price of gold tends not to fall below, while resistance is a level where the price tends not to rise any further. If you can identify these levels on a chart, you will be able to make more informed decisions about when to buy or sell.

In addition to support and resistance levels, it's helpful to know other technical indicators, such as moving averages. These are lines that show the average price of gold over a certain period of time, such as 50 or 200 days. When the price of gold crosses above or below a moving average, it can be a sign that a new trend is beginning. Some traders also use the "relative strength index" (RSI), which measures whether gold is overbought or oversold. If the RSI shows that gold is overbought, the price may soon fall, and if it's oversold, it can be a sign that the price is going to rise. Using these indicators allows you to make more informed decisions based on real data, rather than relying solely on instinct or emotion.

Speaking of emotions, another key secret to gold trading is learning to control them. One of the biggest mistakes traders make, both beginners and experienced, is letting emotions cloud their judgment. Fear and greed are the two emotions that affect traders the most. For example, it's easy to feel fear when the market moves against you and sell out early, missing out on the chance of a recovery. Likewise, greed can cause you to hold on to a trade that has been profitable for a long time, hoping to make more, only to see the market turn around and end up losing what you had made. That's why an important secret to being successful in gold trading is to be disciplined. Setting clear boundaries for when to enter and exit a trade, and sticking to them no matter what happens, is key to avoiding making impulsive decisions that can cost you money.

One tool that many successful traders use to prevent their emotions from getting in the way is the "stop loss." A stop loss is an automatic order that closes a trade when the price reaches a predetermined level, thereby limiting losses. For example, if you buy gold at $1,900 an ounce, you can set a stop loss at $1,850. If the price drops to that level, your trade will automatically close, limiting your losses. This way, you don't have to worry about constantly monitoring the market, and you can protect your capital from sudden moves. Experienced traders also often use the "take profit," which is the opposite of the stop loss: an order that closes your trade when the price reaches a predetermined profit level. This allows you to ensure that you exit the market with a profit, without letting greed keep you waiting too long.

Another secret to gold trading is to diversify your strategies. Don't limit yourself to just one way of trading. For example, you can do short-term trading, buying and selling gold on the same day, taking advantage of small movements in the price. This is a strategy that can generate quick profits, but it is also riskier, as it requires constant monitoring of the market. Another option is long-term trading, where you hold your positions for weeks or months, hoping that the price will rise significantly. This approach is usually more relaxed and less stressful, but it requires patience and trust that the market will move in your favor over time.

Also, it's important not to put all your resources into one trade. Many traders make the mistake of investing too much capital into a single position, which leaves them exposed to large losses if the market moves against them. The key is to spread your capital across multiple trades and strategies. This not only protects you from significant losses, but also allows you to take advantage of different opportunities in the market. If one trade doesn't go well, others can make up for those losses.

It is also critical to be aware of long-term trends in the gold market. While the price of gold can be volatile in the short term, over the long term it tends to follow more predictable patterns. For example, during times of high inflation, gold tends to rise in price as investors seek to protect themselves against currency losses. On the other hand, when interest rates are high, gold may lose appeal as investors prefer assets that generate higher returns. Staying informed about these trends will allow you to make smarter decisions and avoid trading against the natural flow of the market.

Another secret to success in gold trading is to constantly educate yourself. Financial markets are constantly changing, and what worked a few years ago may not be effective today. Read books, take courses, follow experienced traders, and stay abreast of global news and events that may affect the gold market. The more you know, the better equipped you will be to make informed decisions and adapt to changing market conditions.

Finally, one of the most important secrets of gold trading is patience. Gold can be volatile in the short term, but in the long term it tends to follow more predictable patterns. Don't despair if your first few trades aren't successful or if the market doesn't move the way you expected. Learning to be patient and wait for the right time to enter and exit the market is one of the most valuable skills a trader can develop.

In short, success in gold trading is not about discovering a magic trick, but about applying a combination of smart strategies, emotional control and discipline. Gold is a valuable and versatile asset, but it can also be unpredictable. Learning to read the market, diversifying your investments, controlling your emotions and always being willing to learn are the real secrets to success in gold trading.

How to Get Rich Trading Gold

Getting rich from gold trading is a goal that many people pursue, but like any important financial goal, it takes time, effort, and a well-thought-out strategy. While it's true that gold can be a profitable investment, it's not a quick path to riches. To achieve this goal, you need to have a plan, constantly learn, and know how to make the most of the opportunities that this market offers. In this chapter, I'll explain how you can turn gold trading into a source of wealth, using clear and simple strategies that have worked for many successful traders.

The first step to getting rich trading gold is to understand that it is a continuous learning process. Gold, like any other asset, constantly fluctuates in price, and those fluctuations are influenced by a number of factors that you must learn to interpret. It is not simply a matter of buying gold when it is cheap and selling it when it goes up, but rather understanding why it goes up or down, and how you can get ahead of those movements. This involves studying the financial markets, knowing the factors that affect gold (such as inflation, interest rates, and geopolitics), and always keeping an eye on global news. Gold is an asset that is very sensitive to economic and political changes, and learning to read those signals will give you a huge advantage.

One of the secrets to making money trading gold is having a solid strategy and following it in a disciplined manner. Many beginner traders make the mistake of trading without a plan, going with instinct or emotion. This approach rarely works in the long run. If you want to get rich trading gold, you need to set clear rules about when to buy, when to sell, and how much you are willing to risk on each trade. For example, a common rule is to never risk more than 1% or 2% of your capital on a single trade. This way, even if the market moves against you, your losses will be manageable, and you will be able to continue trading in the future.

Risk management is key to building wealth through gold trading. Even the most experienced traders don't win every trade, but what separates them from the unsuccessful ones is how they handle their losses. Instead of trying to quickly recoup lost money, successful traders accept losses as part of the process and stick with their strategy. A very useful tool for managing risk is the use of stop-loss orders, which automatically close a trade if the price of gold falls below a certain level. This protects you from excessive losses and allows you to preserve your capital for future opportunities.

Another important aspect of getting rich from gold trading is to diversify your investments. While gold can be an excellent source of income, you shouldn't put all your money into this one asset. Diversifying means investing in different financial instruments besides gold, such as stocks, bonds, or real estate, so that if one market isn't performing well, the others can make up for those losses. Even within the gold market, there are several ways to invest, such as buying physical gold, trading futures, or investing in gold ETFs. By diversifying your strategies within the gold market and across other sectors, you can reduce risk and increase your chances of generating sustainable profits.

The next crucial step to getting rich trading gold is to maintain a long-term mindset. While it is possible to make quick profits in trading, true riches accumulate over time. The most successful traders don't seek to get rich overnight. Instead, they build their fortune by trading consistently and in a disciplined manner for years. Each trade is part of a larger plan to grow their capital, and they never risk everything on a single move. This long-term approach will also allow you to take advantage of broader trends in the gold market, such as price increases during periods of inflation or economic crises.

To get rich trading gold, you also need to learn to be patient. One of the most common mistakes among traders is impatience – the desire to make big profits quickly. This mindset can lead to making impulsive decisions, such as entering trades when the market is at its highest or selling too soon when things get tough. While it's important to keep an eye out for opportunities, patience is key to waiting for the right moments to act. Remember that gold is an asset that tends to increase in value over time, and sometimes it's better to wait for a temporary correction or dip rather than rush in.

Another key aspect of building wealth through gold trading is reinvesting your profits. Instead of immediately spending the profits you make from a successful trade, many smart traders reinvest that money to grow their capital. This "compounding" strategy allows you to harness the power of compound interest, meaning that the more you invest, the faster your wealth will grow over time. For example, if you start with an initial capital of $10,000 and earn a 10% return, you will have $11,000. If you reinvest that $11,000 and earn another 10%, your capital will be $12,100, and so on. This approach of reinvesting your profits can greatly accelerate the growth of your wealth.

One of the advantages of gold trading is that you can start with relatively little capital and build your wealth gradually. Unlike other markets, such as real estate, where a considerable initial investment is needed, gold trading can be done with smaller sums. This allows you to start without excessive risk, learn over time, and increase your capital as you gain more experience. However, it is important not to underestimate the importance of constantly educating yourself. The world of trading is constantly changing, and strategies that work today might not work tomorrow. Therefore, one of the most important steps to getting rich from gold trading is to invest in your education, read books, take courses, and stay on top of market trends.

Technology also plays a crucial role in successful gold trading. Today, there are numerous trading tools and platforms that allow you to trade efficiently and make decisions based on accurate data. From advanced charts to real-time analysis, modern trading platforms provide you with everything you need to analyze the market and execute your trades effectively. Taking advantage of these technological tools can make the difference between success and failure in gold trading. Additionally, the use of mobile apps and automated systems allows you to place trades even when you are not in front of a computer, giving you an edge in a market that operates 24 hours a day.

One aspect that you should not overlook if you want to get rich from gold trading is to keep an eye on signals from central banks. Central banks are key players in the gold market as their decisions on interest rates, gold reserves, and monetary policy can have a significant impact on the price of gold. When central banks raise interest rates, the price of gold tends to go down as investors prefer assets that generate higher returns. On the other hand, when central banks lower rates or buy large amounts of gold, the price tends to go up. Being aware of these movements will give you an edge when deciding when to enter or exit the market.

Finally, to get rich trading gold, you must learn to be resilient. Trading is not an easy or obstacle-free path. There will be times when the market does not move in your favor, and you will face losses. However, successful traders know how to overcome these challenges and keep moving forward. They do not let setbacks discourage them and instead see them as learning opportunities. Every mistake is a lesson, and every loss is an opportunity to improve your skills. The key is to not give up, stay disciplined, and keep working on your strategy until you see results.

In short, getting rich from gold trading is no easy task, but with the right strategies, proper discipline, and a long-term approach, it is entirely possible. Learn as much as you can about the market, set a solid plan, control your emotions, and be patient. If you follow these principles, you will be on the right path to achieving financial success through gold trading.

www.ingramcontent.com/pod-product-compliance
Lightning Source LLC
Chambersburg PA
CBHW051223160726
47994CB00002B/728